Buying Cars for Really Smart People

From Advance Preparation To Negotiating A Great Deal, To Surviving Finance and Insurance, This Book Is A Simple Car Buying Guide For Everyone

by Jeffrey G. Yonek, J.D.

DORRANCE
PUBLISHING CO
EST. 1920
PITTSBURGH, PENNSYLVANIA 15238

Dorrance Publishing Co
585 Alpha Drive
Pittsburgh, PA 15238
Visit our website at *www.dorrancebookstore.com*

ISBN: 979-8-8852-7001-4
eISBN: 979-8-8852-7731-0

Buying Cars for Really Smart People

From Advance Preparation To Negotiating A Great Deal, To Surviving Finance and Insurance, This Book Is A Simple Car Buying Guide For Everyone

Acknowledgements

I want to thank all my family and friends, especially my lovely wife Jody and my children, who I am blessed and honored to have in my life. Without you, I would not be the person I am today. Thank you.

Limitation of Liability & Disclaimer of All Warranties

The author and publisher of this book make no representations or warranties regarding accuracy and/or the contents of this book, and disclaim any and all warranties whatsoever. The author and publisher shall not be liable for any damages whatsoever arising from the contents of this book or the implementation of the strategies herein. The strategies and ideas in this book are not meant to constitute legal or other professional advice in any way whatsoever. The strategies and ideas in this book may not be suitable for every car buying situation. Results may vary. The laws of each state and municipality may differ and could affect your car buying experience. If you feel you need legal or other professional services, then you should seek the advice of licensed professionals.

Any reference to websites in this book shall not be considered an endorsement of that website or company by the author or publisher, nor do the author and publisher guaranty the accuracy of the information contained within the websites referenced herein. These websites are constantly changing and may cease to exist at any time.

Table of Contents

Introduction xi

Chapter 1: Do Your Research Before Going to the Dealership 1

Research Which Vehicle You Want to Buy
Research Prices on the Vehicle You Want to Buy
Research the Value of Your Trade
Clean Your Trade Before Going to the Dealership

Chapter 2: Negotiating at the Dealership 7

Go for a Test Drive
Ask for the CARFAX Report
Negotiate the Purchase Price of Your New Car or Truck and Your Trade
Always Be Willing to Walk
Dealer Holdback
Dealer Documentary Service Fee
Monthly Payments vs. Purchase Price
Interest Rate on Your Loan
    Buy Rate

Chapter 3: Finance & Insurance (Signing Final Paperwork) 15

Interest Rate on Your New Loan
Subprime Financing
First Payment Due Date
Dealer Add-Ons
    Extended Warranties
    Key Fob Insurance
    VIN Etching
    Interior Protection Package
GAP Insurance

GAP Insurance Refunds
Pre-filled in Charges/Adjustments

Chapter 4: Servicing Your Vehicle **22**
Up-Sell
    Engine and Cabin Air Filters
    Tire Rotation
    Alignment
Call Ahead for Estimate
Dealer Service/Parts Discount Coupons

Conclusion **26**
Cheat Sheet **27**

Introduction

Have you ever wondered whether you got taken to the cleaners by the dealership where you just purchased your new or used car? Ever thought, *What did I just do?* I have. Did you just overpay for a mediocre car and finance it at an exorbitantly high interest rate? Or did you squeeze every last shiny copper penny out of the dealer and feel good doing it? I have done that too.

The goal of this book is to walk you through the many aspects of buying a car. Knowing how dealers make their money will help you understand how to pay them less. If you want to get a good—no, great—deal on buying a new/used car or truck and feel really good about it, then this is the book for you.

I have made numerous mistakes buying cars over the past decades, but I learn from each mistake and get a better deal the next time. I have purchased around 50 cars throughout my life, so that is a lot of mistakes and lessons learned! We're only human. We commit a series of mistakes over our lifetime, and that's okay, so long as we learn from each and every one of them.

The purpose of this book is to share with you many of the mistakes I have made and knowledge gained along the way, so you do not make the same mistakes. If you learn anything from my somewhat vast car buying experience, then you should save lots of money over the course of your lifetime.

Keep in mind that all automobile dealerships are different, and many states have different laws that can affect your purchase of a car or truck. The purpose of this book is to provide you with a general roadmap on how to navigate the various aspects of purchasing a new or used vehicle. If you prepare in advance and implement one or more of the suggestions in this book, then you should save some money. If you do that, then I have done my job.

Here's a tip to get you started and to keep in mind throughout the process: Always be respectful and courteous. I have found that you get more with honey than with vinegar.

Chapter 1

Do Your Research Before Going To The Dealership

Knowledge is power. Do your research in advance. Know what you want and how much you are willing to pay before visiting the dealership. Knowing what car or truck you want to buy (new or used) and how much you are willing to pay before you go to the dealership will give you the confidence to insist on a good, if not great, deal. You also should know what to expect for your trade, if you have one.

If you do not get the deal you want, then leave. Being willing to get up and walk out with confidence will bring you immense power to negotiate a deal you will be happy with. I have even had salesmen run after my car as I was driving out of the dealership parking lot. I stopped in the road and asked him if he was ready to sell me a car. He said yes, and I got a great deal.

If you ever have to get up and walk out, tell the sales rep to sharpen his or her pencil. When they are ready to sell you a car, they can call or text you. If they don't, then it's their loss. Never, ever get emotionally attached to one particular car. There are lots of cars and trucks out there.

Determining which car or truck to buy is very important. If you show up at a dealership without knowing exactly what vehicle you want to buy and how much you are willing to pay, the sales rep will waste lots of time showing you overpriced cars or trucks you are not interested in. If you have done your research and know in advance what you want, then you will not waste time or money at the dealership. If you are looking for a used car and the dealer does not have what you want, respectfully thank them for their time and leave. Do not let them talk you into something you did not research nor want.

Determining what to buy is not as complicated as it might seem. You should focus on *value, quality, and reliability*. Some brands have reputations for excelling in one or more of these categories. Conduct your research focusing on these topics. Begin your search with vehicle reviews.

One of the websites I like to use is Kelley Blue Book (www.kbb.com). I have found that KBB is fairly easy to navigate without going to third party sites, so I will begin by focusing on research using that website. Start by clicking on the "Car Reviews" tab at the top of the page. Select "Top 10 Lists" to begin your search. Although these lists focus on new cars and trucks, you can get a pretty good sense of a manufacturer's reputation. Conduct more than one search. Also use general websites such as Google or Duck Duck Go. Be careful not to click on a third party paid advertisement that pops up during your search.

Another website I like is www.edmunds.com. There is a "Car Reviews" tab at the top right side of the home page. This website has a top 10 list for just about every vehicle category. The reviews list the pros and cons of each rated vehicle, along with what is new for the model year. The ratings also provide information on drivability, comfort, interior, technology, storage, value, and how economical the vehicle is.

Once you decide on which car or truck to buy, then it's time to research what your favorite vehicle sells for, so you know roughly how much you will pay at the dealership. By doing this, you can determine which options you want; what model year to buy; and how much mileage you are willing to accept on a vehicle based on your budget.

Be very careful not to buy a vehicle with higher mileage; low mileage is best. If you cannot afford a vehicle with low mileage, you need to know that a higher mileage car will come with much higher maintenance costs. You might want to consider a lower mileage car or truck that is a year or two older to stay within your budget.

Research Prices on the Vehicle You Want to Buy

Now it's time to begin your vehicle search. Start by visiting car buying sites such as Auto Trader, Car Gurus, or Edmunds.com. You can find them at www.autotrader.com, www.cargurus.com, and www.edmunds .com, respectively.

Input the parameters you desire in a vehicle, such as year, mileage and a dealer located within so many miles of your zip code. Auto Trader and Edmunds will provide you with "Great Price" or "Good Price" commentary based on the advertised price for each vehicle. Car Gurus will give you a "Great Deal," "Good Deal," or "Fair Deal" evaluation of their vehicle offerings. A dealer's internet price is often that dealer's best price, or at least something fairly close to it. Usually, it is much lower than a "walk in off the street" retail asking price.

After you have narrowed down your vehicle search, you are able to determine what is available and how much dealers are asking. This will help you figure out how much money to spend on a particular car or truck.

Once you find a particular vehicle located near you that you are interested in, reach out to the dealer with the contact information provided in the ad. This should connect you directly with the dealership's internet department, where you will receive by far the best price. Once you confirm the vehicle has the options you like, have the sales rep email you their best price for that particular vehicle. Print the email out and take it with you when you go to the dealership. That way, if you are placed with a different sales rep and he quotes you a higher price, simply show him your email, so you both are on the same page.

Find identical or similar vehicles at two different dealerships that have the same options. Get the best internet price from both dealerships. Make sure you are comparing apples to apples, not apples to oranges. Visit the lowest price dealership first. If you are not able to make a deal, then you have a backup second dealer to visit.

Research the Value of Your Trade

Now that you have completed your research on the new/used vehicle you would like to purchase, it's time to research the value of your trade. Many people only focus on what they are paying for a new car. As a result, they lose focus on the other half of the transaction— getting a great price for your trade.

Although you want to get the highest possible price for your trade, you still have to be realistic. Expect to receive "trade in value" for your car or truck. A dealer will not pay you private party or retail value for your trade. Remember, if you are not realistic, you are wasting your time. So let's get started.

Although I like to use the Kelley Blue Book valuation tools, there are many other websites on the internet with valuation tools. On the Kelley Blue Book home page, click on the "Car Values" tab at the top of the page and then the "My Car's Value" tab in the drop-down box. Input the particulars of the vehicle you are trading in.

When you get to the "What is your vehicle's condition?" page, be realistic about the condition of your vehicle. Almost none of the vehicles traded in are in excellent condition. Most cars are in "good" or "very good" condition. Your report will provide you with a trade-in value range on your vehicle for the options and condition you select. The condition of your trade is very important when establishing the value of your trade.

If your trade is in less than fair condition, you might want to sell your car in a private sale and purchase your new or used car without a trade. You would, however, pay more for sales tax if your state reduces the sales tax by the value of your trade (sales tax credit). This is something to consider when deciding whether to trade in your car or sell it in a private sale. Trading in your car with a dealer is much easier, however.

Once you get your trade's value, print out both the "good" and "very good" reports for your car. Take them with you in a folder to the dealership. Your sales rep will see that you have done your research and will not waste your time, or at least not nearly as much of it. Make an offer on how much you want to be paid for your trade. So you have room to negotiate, offer a little more than the trade in value in your report. Depending on the value of your trade, make the dealer an offer which is $1,000-$2,000 above the trade in value of your trade.

In a recent car buying experience, the sales rep told me my trade was in near excellent condition after he inspected it, so I knew the "very good" value report was accurate. After I made an offer on what I expected to receive for my trade, the salesman left and came back five minutes later with a valuation report showing a value on my trade thousands of dollars below my offer. He convincingly told me I needed to be more reasonable and that the report is what dealers pay for trades similar to my car. After I reviewed the salesman's valuation report, I noticed that he printed out a report for my vehicle with a "FAIR" condition (the lowest possible condition on Kelley Blue Book).

The condition category is usually in very small print, but it should be on the report. If you do not see it, ask your sales rep what condition they used to value your trade. I ever so respectfully called my salesman on his "fair" condition selection and asked him to "humor me" and bring me a report on my car with a "very good" condition report. He came back a minute later with the correct "very good" report, and the valuation was about $3,000 higher. I told him THAT was what I would accept for my trade, and he said yes! Remember, knowledge is power, and this single point might possibly yield potential savings of hundreds or even thousands of dollars in your transaction.

Clean Your Trade Before You Go to the Dealership

It's really simple: Clean your trade before you go to the dealership. Wash the outside; vacuum the inside; clean the windows; and wipe down your dashboard. A good first impression has value. If your car looks like a pig pen, the value of your trade will suffer. If you fail to do this in advance, you are swimming against the tide on the value of your trade at the dealership.

Chapter 2

Negotiating At The Dealership

Having completed your research, you now are ready to visit the dealership. You are armed with your research. You are familiar with the brands and options you like; you know what you want and how much you expect to pay; and how much you expect to receive for your trade, realistically. Remember that knowledge is power. Take your research with you, as you most likely will need it.

Go For a Test Drive

Before you start negotiating, take a test drive in the car or truck you want to buy. Do not get emotionally attached to any vehicle. Do not feel you have to buy that particular car. If you are not successful in negotiating a great deal, feel free to leave. At this point in the process, you have absolutely no obligation to buy a car or truck from the dealership, no matter how much pressure the dealer exerts on you. You are only interested in buying the right car *for the right price* (and right trade in value as well). Make sure the sales rep knows you are in no rush to buy a vehicle.

After your test drive, if you notice any defects or issues with the vehicle you want to be fixed before you buy the car or truck, be sure to include it in writing with your offer to buy the vehicle. When signing final paperwork, you almost always sign a piece of paper confirming that the dealership owes you nothing (or something) additional on the vehicle. That's why it is so important to document any items that must be addressed on the vehicle you are buying *before* you make a deal. Most dealers are not willing to make major repairs on a vehicle, but depending on the item, it may result in an additional price reduction.

Ask for the Carfax Report

If you are buying a used car or truck, after you test drive the vehicle you want to buy, ask the dealer for the CARFAX report on that particular vehicle. This will show you any accidents and resulting damage to the vehicle, structural or otherwise. The CARFAX report also will show you any title deficiencies, such as flood or total loss; accident data and service history; type of use (such as whether the vehicle was a rental car or taxi); and ownership history (previous owners, length of ownership, and last reported mileage). You can visit the website at www.carfax.com to pull your own CARFAX report on a particular vehicle, though you will have to pay for the report if you do not get it from a dealer.

Accidents with structural damage, flood, or total loss designations will significantly decrease a vehicle's value, both when you buy the car and, more importantly, when you decide to sell it. Any of these designations could result in a few, or even several, thousand-dollar deduction on the value of the vehicle, so be aware and try to stay away from those vehicles. They can be mechanical nightmares and valuation pits. You will lose money on these vehicles in the long run, no matter how nice they look and how cheap they are. Stay away from them.

Years ago, I knowingly purchased a vehicle with a CARFAX report that showed an accident with structural damage to the car. The vehicle was expertly repaired and looked great. I bought the car at about a $4,000 discount, knowing it had that CARFAX history. I never had any mechanical issues, but when I went to sell the car almost two years later, a dealer wanted to pay me about $10,000 less for my trade. He said that he was not willing to take any risk whatsoever on my car. He was going to wholesale out my car to another dealer. He eventually increased his offer by $4,000, but still, that was not enough. I walked and sold the car on the private market several weeks later with full disclosure of the accident for a few thousand dollars more, though still for a very fair price considering then current market conditions. I strongly suggest, based on my own experience, not to buy a vehicle with a bad CARFAX history.

Negotiate the Purchase Price of Your New Car or Truck and Your Trade

After you test drive the vehicle you want to buy, make an offer on that vehicle. Do not offer what you expect to pay. Depending on the price of the vehicle you want to buy, offer the sales rep $2,000 or more *less* than what you want to pay. That way, you have room to negotiate. If he looks at you like you just landed from Mars, tell him that's your offer.

You also will tell the sales rep what you want for your trade. You have done the research. You have the Kelley Blue Book reports which tell you the "Good" and "Very Good" values on your trade. Begin by considering your vehicle as "Very Good," even if it is only in "Good" condition, as this is a subjective opinion. Without showing the sales rep your research, offer a dollar amount that is $1,000-$2,000 more than the "Very Good" condition in your report. Again, that way, you leave room to negotiate.

Expect to negotiate on both the purchase price of the new or used car you want to buy and the value of your trade. Ultimately, you will pay a net amount, which is the difference between the new car purchase price less the value of your trade. If you still have a car loan on your trade, then the amount of your existing car loan will be added to your new loan balance.

After you make your offer, the sales rep will take your offer to his floor manager. He will return in five to 10 minutes. I believe they take their time so your anticipation builds and you want the car even more. Don't let that happen to you. Simply expect to wait for his return and think nothing of it.

The sales rep most likely will present to you a value report on your trade and tell you your trade in value expectation is far too high. That is when you look for the value condition ("Fair," "Good," or "Very Good") on his report. If it is not there, ask him what value he used to calculate your trade value. Remember that the "Fair" condition always results in a much lower value for your trade. This is when you ask him to "humor me" and to bring you a report using the "very good" value. Be honest with yourself; if your trade realistically is in "good" condition only, then ask for that report instead. Most dealers will not falsify a Kelley Blue Book valuation report. But they are willing to use the "Fair" value report for their initial trade offers, notwithstanding the true condition of your car. Most people do not understand that this can make a big difference in the value of your trade.

When the sales rep comes back, he should have the accurate valuation report on your vehicle. You will see that results in a higher value for your trade. Now you are in a position to make a counteroffer using a higher value for your trade, closer to what you are expecting to receive. Your goal is to get at least as much as the Kelley Blue Book trade in value for your car, maybe a little more, depending on your vehicle, its condition, and current market conditions.

While you and the sales rep have been negotiating back and forth, a floor manager would have obtained your keys and taken your car for a test drive. They still have the keys. They purposely do not bring back your keys and hand them over. They usually keep your keys as a tactic to get you to stay and make a deal.

If you have made two offers (for both purchase price on your new/used vehicle and your trade) without reaching a deal, tell the sales rep to bring back your keys. At this point, usually the floor manager brings back your keys, and he makes a final push for a deal. You can tell him that you might be flexible with a few hundred dollars, but that he also needs to "sharpen *his* pencil." Make him a final offer. Let him know that you are ready to leave and that you are not in a hurry to buy a car.

If the sales rep does not accept your offer, grab your keys, politely tell him, "Thank you for your time," and walk. If the manager asks if you are willing to lose out over a few hundred dollars, tell him that you are surprised *he* is willing to lose a sale over a few hundred dollars. They usually are not.

Dealer Holdback

If you are a couple thousand dollars away from a deal and you are ready to leave, that's usually when the sales rep or manager sometimes will offer to show you his dealer invoice on the vehicle (this only relates to new vehicles). This typically is the price the dealer paid for the car or truck from the manufacturer. This is how a dealer demonstrates to you that he is not making very much money on your offer, which might not necessarily be true.

However, the dealer is banking on you not knowing about "Dealer Holdback." Holdback is a direct payment the dealer receives from the automobile manufacturer, usually on a quarterly basis. It is paid to the dealer on every new vehicle the dealership sells, usually two to three percent of the retail price. Holdback is designed to supplement the dealer's income by artificially inflating a new vehicle cost to the dealership. If you believe that you are paying at or below the dealer wholesale price on a new vehicle based on dealer invoice, then you still may be leaving money on the table.

Although many dealers will not negotiate away their holdback, your knowledge of the existence of the dealer holdback may provide you with more negotiating power. Besides, the sales rep or manager at least knows you are a knowledgeable buyer and not to waste your time and cut right to their bottom line on the car or truck you want to buy.

If you still are a few thousand dollars away from a deal after two or three offers, then you need to walk. Respectfully tell the sales rep to call or text you when he is ready to sell a car.

If you are less than a thousand dollars from reaching a deal, then make one last offer to split the difference. But make sure the sales rep knows that this is not the beginning of another round of negotiation. You are ready to leave. If the manager comes back and offers you less than splitting the difference at 50/50, meaning much better for the dealership than you, then tell him you will accept his offer ONLY if he eliminates the $150 dealer documentary service fee (assessed at the time of signing the final paperwork); he includes all-weather floor mats at no additional charge; and he fills your tank with gas. Then, and only then, he has a deal. Otherwise, it's time to walk. Make sure any of these last-minute changes are included in your written offer.

Dealer Documentary Service Fee

The $150 dealer documentary service fee is a negotiable fee you pay when you sign the final papers. Negotiate that fee away now, not when signing final paperwork. This is a negotiable fee, though few, if any, car buyers negotiate it away. If the manager or sales rep tells you he has no control over the assessment of that fee, which is not true, then tell him you need an additional $150 off the purchase price of the vehicle you are buying or $150 more for your trade. Be relentless. You will prevail and you will save money.

Monthly Payments Versus Purchase Price

During the course of your negotiation, if the sales rep or manager asks what monthly payments you can handle, let him know that, ultimately, the most important thing is to pay a fair price for the vehicle and to get a fair price for your trade. Monthly payments are secondary. Paying too much for a new or used car means you will have more debt to pay off over time.

If you pay too much for a new vehicle, the dealer usually can finance your purchase over six years, resulting in a lower monthly payment. Don't be fooled by this; the problem with lower payments on a six or even a five-year loan is that your car might always be worth less than the amount you owe on the car loan. That's why it is important to get a great deal in the first place. Never forget that.

Interest Rate on Your Loan

The interest rate on your loan will be a reflection of your credit worthiness. If you have great credit, a lender will loan you the funds to purchase your new vehicle at a lower interest rate. If, on the other hand, you have marginal credit, lenders will only offer financing at a higher interest rate. The lower your credit score, the higher your interest rate will be. Keep in mind that it will take longer to pay off a higher interest rate loan since your monthly payment usually pays off accrued interest first.

Buy Rate

When you are negotiating your deal with the sales rep, make sure he knows that as a part of your deal, you insist on financing at the "Buy Rate." If you have very good to excellent credit, you have the power to negotiate the interest rate you will pay on your car loan. Just remember that the interest rate is a reflection of your credit worthiness, so this only works if you have great credit.

The buy rate is the actual interest rate on which the lender is willing to loan you the money to finance your new/used vehicle purchase. For example, if the bank is willing to finance your vehicle purchase at 4 percent, then that is the buy rate. Typically, the dealer will offer you financing at a rate higher than the buy rate. If the dealer writes your vehicle loan at an interest rate higher than the buy rate, such as 5 percent, then the dealership is paid additional money by the bank in the form of a yield spread premium. The higher the yield spread, the more money the dealer receives from the bank to finance your car purchase. Dealers make lots of money this way. Do not let them make any money on *your* car loan.

Your job here is to not let the dealer make that extra revenue on your loan. When you are negotiating back and forth with the sales rep, make sure each written offer includes financing at the buy rate. If your credit is not good enough for you to receive a loan at the buy rate, make sure your offer includes a notation that the final deal is subject to interest rate approval by buyer. This means that you are not going to agree to financing at any interest rate, especially a high interest rate. When you go to sign final papers, you can decide if the interest rate is acceptable to you. If your credit score is not very good, you have less negotiating power, if any, on the interest rate.

Chapter 3

Finance And Insurance (Signing Final Paperwork)

Now that you have negotiated a great deal on both your trade and the purchase price of your new/used car or truck, it's not over yet. You still have to sign the final paperwork with the Finance & Insurance (F&I) Department. Stay vigilant; there still is lots to be aware of at this point in the transaction.

Interest Rate on Your New Loan

Most people just accept the interest rate the F&I manager tells them they will be paying for their car loan. I did that for many years until I finally discovered that I had the power to negotiate the interest rate on my loan. Negotiate down the interest rate even a half percentage point, and you will save hundreds, if not thousands, of dollars over the course of your loan. Your power to negotiate the interest rate dwindles with a lower or marginal credit score.

If you already agreed as part of your deal that you only will pay the buy rate, then remind the F&I manager and confirm that your loan interest rate is, in fact, the agreed buy rate. If you have no such agreement as part of your deal, then simply tell the F&I manager that his offered rate is too high and to look for better rates with different lenders. Sometimes they can find a better, more competitive rate that lowers your monthly payment.

Subprime Financing

Remember, your interest rate will be a reflection of your credit score. If you have marginal or bad credit, your only option might be subprime financing. Subprime interest rates are extremely high and can be as much as 25 percent or higher. If you agree to subprime financing, a larger portion of your monthly payment will first pay the higher interest, and therefore, it will take longer for you to pay off your loan.

Another problem with subprime financing is that your loan balance is often higher than the value of your car or truck. This makes it very difficult to sell or trade your vehicle in the future. Nevertheless, subprime financing is legal in many states and it has a legitimate place in auto financing.

First Payment Due Date

If the F&I manger tells you that your first payment is not due for six to eight weeks, ask him to recalculate your loan with a first payment due date that is much sooner (maybe three weeks or more). By shortening the time for your first payment, your monthly payment will be reduced by at least a few dollars every month because less interest accrues over time. Every little bit of savings helps.

At the time you sign final paperwork in the Finance & Insurance Department, most dealerships offer optional add-ons at an additional cost to your vehicle purchase price. These items are highly profitable for the dealer. Many add-ons can be purchased from other venders where they often will cost much less, but some are exclusive to the dealer. Common dealer add-ons include extended warranties, key fob insurance, VIN etching, credit life or disability insurance, windshield chip insurance, and Interior Protection Package, to name a few.

Here is the basic and most important thing to remember about dealer add-ons: NEVER, EVER, EVER agree to buy *any* dealer add-ons. Don't waste the money you just saved by negotiating a great deal. *Just say no!* I'll say it again: Never, ever spend money on dealer add-ons.

The F&I manager will first make you think they are a great deal and that once you leave the dealership, they will not be available to you again. Okay; that's fine. If you stand firm and refuse, he or she will try to make you feel stupid if you do not purchase any add-ons. Stay strong and be confident. If he asks you why, simply tell him you are just not interested. You do not have to give him a reason. Otherwise, you will be drawn into a debate you cannot win. Tell him that you just want to sign the paperwork and be on your way. No add-ons.

If he tells you the add-ons only increase your monthly payment by a seemingly small amount, ask him what the total cost of the add-ons would be over the life of your loan (or at least how much the additional lump sum cost is). Once you learn the total cost, you will not be interested. Just say no!

Be aware that the dealer might even try to negotiate down the price of their add-ons. It gets tempting, but don't do it. If you are drawn into negotiating the price of add-ons, you are losing sight of your main goal—to get a great deal on your vehicle purchase. So remember, just say no!

Here are a few examples of dealer add-ons:

Extended Warranties

Extended warranties extend the life of your vehicle's warranty, though the coverage may be more restrictive or cover less than a manufacturer's warranty. These warranties are very expensive (sometimes a few thousand dollars) and will rarely pay for themselves. Most extended warranties only fix certain items, so when you have a breakdown after your manufacturer's warranty has run out, you may or may not be covered. Many extended warranties have deductibles which water down the value of the product. Overall, they are not a good deal. Stay away from them.

Key Fob Insurance

Many newer vehicles have expensive key fobs for unlocking the doors and some even act as a proximity key to remotely start the car. If you lose one of your key fobs, it may cost a few hundred dollars to replace. Key fob insurance usually costs *several* hundred dollars. You might have to lose two or three key fobs just *to break even*. This type of insurance sounds good, but it is not a good value. Just say no!

VIN Etching

Vehicle Identification Number (VIN) etching imprints the VIN on your vehicle's windows. VIN etching may or may not be a theft deterrent, but there is no need to pay a dealership $200-$300 for a service when you can purchase a VIN etching kit on Amazon for around one tenth of that amount. If you absolutely have to have VIN etching, do it yourself and save money.

Interior Protection Package

This add-on is a chemical treatment applied to your vehicle's upholstery and carpet to waterproof and protect it from stains. Some dealers charge up to $200 or more for this package. I prefer to buy a $10 can of Scotchgard from Walmart and do it myself.

GAP Insurance

GAP insurance may be the only dealer add-on sometimes worth purchasing, especially if you have subprime financing or your new lender requires it. If you only finance a small portion of your vehicle purchase, then this insurance is not for you. On the other hand, if you finance the entire purchase price and sales tax, then you might want to consider GAP coverage. A GAP Addendum can cost upwards of $895, but it might bring peace of mind knowing that you will not have that liability.

Here is how GAP insurance works. If you are in an accident and your car is a total loss, your auto insurance company will only pay you the market value of your vehicle at that time. If you owe more on your car loan than the insurance payment, you are liable to your lender to pay off the remaining balance on your loan. GAP insurance is designed to pay off the remaining balance on your car loan after a total loss accident.

Keep in mind, however, that GAP insurance normally does not cover late or missed payments. This insurance is designed to pay off the remaining balance of your car loan where there are no late or missed payments, no accrued late fees, and no additional interest from late or missed payments. Also be aware of coverage limits in some policies which will cap the amount paid on a claim.

If you purchased a GAP addendum or policy and you sell your car before your car loan is paid off, then you are entitled to a refund of the unused portion of the GAP policy. I sold or traded in many of my cars over the years and never asked for a GAP refund. Nevertheless, you must keep your original paperwork, as you may be required to present it to the dealership when requesting your refund. Make sure you keep these papers in a safe place where you will remember their location.

Read the terms on the back of your GAP contract, and it will tell you what you have to do in order to get a refund on the unused portion of your GAP policy. This usually entails a written request to the dealer (Attention, F&I Department) and a copy of the policy included with your request. It might take four to six weeks to receive your refund. If your policy has clear terms on how to receive a refund and the dealer will not cooperate, threaten to contact your state's dealer division in the department of licensing or the Attorney General. That should get their attention.

Prefilled Charges/Adjustments

Before you sign any of your final paperwork, read the documents, especially where the numbers are filled in, detailing the calculations in your transaction.

One time when I was in finance and insurance signing final paperwork, I actually read the long contract and reviewed the numbers that determine the total amount financed for my new car loan. I saw an entry with an obscure entry of $495 "Price Adjustment." I asked the F&I manager what that was and she said: "Oh, that must have been prefilled and should not be there." She took it out. It seems unlikely to me that a form on *her* computer would have dollar amounts that she did not write in herself. But no worries, the price adjustment was removed, and I saved about $500, which I never agreed to pay in the first place.

The moral of the story? Be vigilant; read the documents, especially the numbers that determine how much you will pay for your new or used car. If you have any questions, be sure to ask. Do not sign anything until you understand the numbers.

Chapter 4
Servicing Your Vehicle

After you get that great deal on your new/used car or truck, do not waste those savings on overpaying for vehicle service. If you bought a new car or truck, it is important to have your vehicle serviced at the dealership in order to stay current with the manufacturer's warranty. If you try to save money and have your car or truck serviced somewhere else, it might be difficult to prove to the dealer that you had the vehicle serviced regularly and correctly if and when warranty work needs to be performed.

However, just because you are going to the dealer to service your vehicle does not mean that you have to overpay for those services. Here are some things to look out for.

Up-Sell

Up-sell is when the dealership service rep talks you into having service done on your vehicle that you either do not need at that time or should not have done at the dealership. The best way to avoid paying for something you do not need is to be familiar with the manufacturer's recommended service schedule for the vehicle you purchased. Extra dealer recommendations mean more money for the dealer and less money in your pocket.

Here are a few examples of up-sell:

Engine and Cabin Air Filters

One of the most common up-sell is overpaying for a cabin or engine air filter that you can buy and install yourself, and save lots of money. A few years ago, I took my car into the dealership where I purchased my new car. I authorized an oil change and tire rotation. After they had my car in the shop, the service rep showed me a dirty cabin air filter and recommended I have it replaced. He also recommended a new engine air filter as well. I was quoted $50 for the two filters and an additional $75 for labor. I asked why the $125 charge for two air filters, and he said that the cabin air filter was behind the dash and it took some time to accomplish the task. I paid the $125...

Never, ever again. Never let the dealer perform this service; do it yourself and save lots of money each time.

I returned home from the dealership and researched the cost of replacement filters on Amazon. I discovered I could buy both filters for about $25 total. Obviously, prices vary by vehicle. I watched a short video on You Tube on how to change the filters. Both tasks combined take about five to 10 minutes, depending on the vehicle. It's really simple.

So the next time the service rep shows you a dirty air filter, tell him you have a spare one at home and that you will install it when you get home. When you return home, order both air filters on Amazon or eBay. Just make sure you order the correct parts by make, model, and year of your vehicle. When you receive the filters in a few days, install them yourself and save $100!

Tire Rotation

Many dealerships will rotate your tires every time you have your oil changed (about every 5,000 miles). The cost usually is about $20. If you purchase your tires from most any tire store after you buy your car, then you might have free rotation for the life of the tires. If that is the case, do not waste money at the dealership if you have free tire rotation service elsewhere.

Alignment

If the service rep tells you they will only do an alignment on your vehicle if it needs it, ask to see the alignment report *before* the work is performed. Have them show it to you and explain why your vehicle needs alignment.

A few years back, a dealer aligned my vehicle when it was in the shop. I looked at the alignment report, and it showed that the vehicle was in perfect alignment. I inquired as to why an alignment was necessary. The service rep disappeared into the service bay and came back a few minutes later with an "explanation." He told me that my steering wheel was slightly off center, so they performed the alignment. I politely advised him that I was not going to pay for a service that my vehicle did not need. They promptly removed the charge from my service bill.

Call Ahead for Estimate

If it is time for one of those expensive 30,000-, 60,000-, or 90,000-mile service visits, call the dealership service department in advance. Ask specifically what is required and how much it will cost. You will most likely get a competitive quote since dealers know that you can shop around and take your business elsewhere. By doing this simple step, you will not be charged more at the service desk. If you are, kindly advise them that you called in advance, you spoke with [insert name here], and your quote was much less. Usually, they will give you a courtesy adjustment to honor that quote.

Many dealerships offer service and/or parts discount coupons online. Research that ahead of time. Print them out and take them with you. Be sure to present your discount coupon to the service rep when they write up your service order. Otherwise, they may not honor the discount if you tell them about your discount after the service was performed.

Conclusion

Remember that knowledge is power. Knowing how dealerships make their money will help you save money on your next vehicle purchase. Do your homework in advance, and be confident in your ability to negotiate a better deal than you would otherwise. Always be respectful, as you will most certainly get more with honey than vinegar. Do this, and you will save money.

Now go and make me proud.

Cheat Sheet When at Dealership

- Value Condition ("Fair," "Good," "Very Good")
- CarFax Report
- Get your keys back after dealer inspects your car
- Always be willing to walk
- Dealer Holdback
- $150 Dealer Doc Fee
- Negotiate interest rate
- Buy Rate (%)
- First payment due date
- NO Dealer Add-Ons
- NO pre-filled charges
- Review all numbers on final paper work before signing